The More I See of Men, The More I Love My Dog

Olivia Edward

Illustrated by Alex Hallatt

summersdale

Front cover design by Anna Prudente, using an illustration by Alex Hallatt.

Illustrations by Alex Hallatt

Colour by Rob Smith

Summersdale Publishers Ltd
46 West Street
Chichester
West Sussex
PO19 1RP
UK

www.summersdale.com

ISBN: 1 84024 266 3
ISBN: 978 1 84024 266 9

Printed and bound by Tien Wah Press, Singapore

For SPF and Thistle

If you are getting fed up with spending all your time searching for the perfect soulmate, or you are thinking of trading in your current partner for a new, improved model, maybe you should think about casting your net closer to home.

A lifelong friend may be nearer than you think … lying curled up in the hall, or making puppy-eyes at you through a window. No, it's not your loony next-door neighbour – a woman's best friend is her dog.

Dogs are better than men. They are much cheaper and more easily replaceable. They won't help around the house, but a cute, well-chosen woofer will open up a whole world of social possibilities. When was the last time someone engaged you in conversation by pointing at your partner and saying, 'Ah, that's a fine looking beast you've got there. Can I stroke him?'

Not yet convinced? You'll be sure to change your mind after reading the following reasons why a furry four-pawed companion is far superior to a flabby flat-footed man.

You won't have to
meet your dog's
mother before you
move in together.

Dogs are always
delighted that you
have graced them
with your company.

Dogs don't come
home angry and
stressed after a
hard day in the park.

Dogs miss you
when you are gone.

You don't need
to spend hours
wondering where
your relationship
with your dog is going.

Dogs don't
expect you to
impress their friends.

Cute dogs
don't know
they are cute.

Dogs are not
excited by a
large pair of
unfamiliar breasts.

Irritating dogs
can be plonked
outside when
you need some
personal space.

Dogs don't
mind when you
put on weight.

Dogs won't
help themselves
to your cash.

You can leave a
dog at home when you
want a wild night out …
and your dog won't
quiz you when you
come in drunk at 3 a.m.
with torn tights.

Dogs feel guilty
and are visibly
remorseful when
they have done
something wrong.

It is highly unlikely that you
will be seized by an overwhelming
desire to take your best friend's
dog home for the night
(but if you do, you can take
it back in the morning and
there will be no hard feelings).

Dogs don't
stay out late
drinking in bars.

Dogs understand when
you are snappy, and
respond accordingly by
offering more affection.

Dogs are not
embarrassed about
expressing their
affection for
you in public.

You never look
at your dog and
wonder whether
you still love them.

Dogs don't need constant
reassurance that you find
them more appealing than
dogs on TV, the dog next
door, dogs at work,
or your best friend's dog.

Dogs know
that you are
always right.

Dogs don't think less of
you for not being able to
understand the offside rule.

A dog will never
criticise your driving
(but most men won't
try to sit on your
lap when you're
at the wheel of your car).

Dogs think that
everything you
feed them is delicious.

Dogs think with
their stomachs.
We all know what
men think with.

Dogs may give
other women
attention, but they
will always come
when they are called.

Dogs don't
point out
when you
have spots.

Dogs know
how to listen.

A dog won't
complain about
your 'dull' friends.

Dogs don't think
you are boring
when you spend
a night in front
of the telly.

Dogs are *always*
happy to see
your family.

Dogs don't feel
insecure because
you earn more
money than they do.

You never wonder
if your dog is
good enough for you.

Dogs make it
very clear if they
want to go out.

Dogs admit
it when they
are jealous.

Dogs understand
the concepts of
commitment and loyalty.

You just *know*
your dog
is The One.

Dogs are not
ashamed to admit
they are lost.

You won't throw a
strop and refuse to
play with your dog
because they always
get too competitive.

Dogs don't
change the subject.

Dogs understand
the meaning of
the word NO.

Dogs know exactly how to behave when you are watching an emotional film: to remain silent and cuddle affectionately without demanding sex or fidgeting.

Dogs don't snigger
at your inability
to throw overarm
when you are
playing Fetch.

Dogs look you in
the eye when you
are speaking to them.

Your dog will not
end your relationship
because they just can't
be the dog you
want them to be.

Dogs can be
housetrained.

Dogs don't resent
your dominant position
in the relationship.

Your dog will continue
to show the greatest
respect for you, even
if you destroy your car's
engine by forgetting to
top up the oil.

To sustain a relationship with your dog, it is not necessary to feign an interest in their hobbies.

Dogs understand that
the correct way to
make up with you is
to be entirely submissive
whilst strongly reaffirming
their love for you.

Dogs sulk quietly in
their beds. They do
not draw attention to
their unhappiness by
huffing loudly and
banging doors.

Dogs don't complain
when you are late.
In fact, they are happier
to see you than if you
had been on time.

Dogs don't bring
other loud, smelly dogs
back to your house
to watch the game.

Dogs make it clear
when they don't like
other dogs. They don't
mutter insults under
their breath.

Dogs don't go
bald in their
senior years.

Dogs don't purchase
flashy sports cars
to prove they are still
young dogs at heart.

If your dog smells
unpleasant or snores
in the night, you
can simply push
them out of bed.

Excitable dogs
can be kept on
tight leads in
public places.

You won't start an
argument with your
dog because they
forgot your birthday.

Dogs don't feel
the need to prove
themselves by jumping
higher, running faster,
or drinking more
water than other dogs.

Dogs don't wear
embarrassing, unfashionable
items of clothing – unless
you want to dress
them in a little red jacket
and matching booties.

With a dog, you don't
have to wait for the right time
before announcing that your
mother is coming to stay.

You won't outgrow
your relationship
with your dog.

Your dog will not feign
knowledge of a subject
they know nothing
about in order to
impress other dogs.

Dogs are not possessive about the TV remote control. They won't touch it unless you throw it across the room in anger. In which case they will bring it back to you.

Dogs don't pretend
the dog they rushed up
to in the park and leapt
on with wild abandon
was just a friend.

Your dog won't run
off with your best
friend … unless you
forget to feed them.

You will never find
yourself in the local
nightclub eyeing up
other dogs and
wishing your dog could
dance like they do.

A dog can be tied
up on shopping trips
so you know you
won't return to find
them browsing
in the hi-fi store.

Fat dogs can be put on diets.
They won't order any sneaky
kebabs when they think
you're not looking.